Business
Plan
Write Now

DETAILED GUIDE TO WRITING A
SUCCESSFUL BUSINESS PLAN

BILL RICHARDSON

Contents

Introduction

Yes. Every business needs a plan.

A plan is needed to guide your business, both now and in the future, to define long-term strategy you'll employ to help you achieve your set goals and mission.

You need a plan to communicate to your employees about where you want to go and how you plan to get there, to motivate them, and direct their activities.

You cannot exclude the business plan if you are planning to seek loan funds, as it is an essential requirement for the process. It will provide potential investors with detailed information on all aspects of the company's past and current operations and provide future projections.

The details contained in a business plan must be concise. Yet, it must provide as much information as possible. And to retain its functional value, it must be duly updated and kept current.

There is no set length to a business plan. The average length runs between 30 to 40 pages, adding the supporting documents section. Depending on the nature of business in question, this can be more or less than the average number of pages.

With the mentioned considerations in mind, you are ready to begin formulating your business plan. Read through this entire guide to get an overall view of the business planning process. This book will lead you step-by-step through the whole process. You'll learn the crucial elements of an effective business plan, as well as the inside tricks and tips that help you sell your business to the people that count—the investors and lenders you depend on for funding.

Chapter One

The Research:

- ❖ Overview

- ❖ Who Writes the Plan?

- ❖ Processes Involved

- ❖ Analyze Your Audience

- ❖ Analyze Your Market

- ❖ Analyze Your Strength

- ❖ Analyze Your Weakness

- ❖ Analyze Your Strategy

Overview of the Business Plan

Most entrepreneurs have very little or no experience in creating business plans. They don't know the information to include in the plan, where to obtain essential information, or how to put them together. They don't know exactly why they're writing a business plan or whom they target with the written plan. If you don't know the why and the whom, you're going to have trouble creating a convincing plan that would make you a kill.

If the above paragraph describes your current state, worry not. You're starting in the exact position as several thousand businesses before you. The difference significant between you and those who came before; the thing that gives you a competitive advantage is that you know what you don't know, and you want to overcome the challenges to create the most effective business plan.

The Components of Ideal Business Plan

You might need to fine-tune this list a bit to suit different types of businesses and their unique circumstances; most business plans will contain some variation of the listed sections:

- **Executive Summary**: This is the first part of the plan, the very first section. It should encapsulate the main points of the entire text in a short (ideally one page), bulleted, easy-to-grasp style.

- **Vision:** This part of the plan, typically just a sentence or a paragraph long at most, expresses your dream for your business; why you're doing what you're doing.

- **Mission:** The Mission is what your business is trying to achieve. Sometimes called a Mission Statement; is a section of short sentence or a paragraph that describes, as clearly as possible, what your business is trying to accomplish.

- **Opportunity:** Sometimes called the Market or Market Dynamics section, it details the compelling reason for your business to exist. Typically, this section includes a wealth of market data that portrays a picture of immense market opportunity.

- **Market Strategy:** This section describes how you'll exploit that tremendous market opportunity described in the previous section, and displays your current and potential market activities, your product development, your marketing, your sales. This section also details your competitors and how you plan to respond to them.

- **Business Strategy:** This section describes the business itself. What you make or sell, and how you intend to make money from doing that(otherwise known as your revenue model).

- **Organization and Operations:** This section may sometimes be broken into separate organizations and Operations sections. It describes your company structure and the backend operations you use to bring your products and services to the market. (This is where you'll heap all sorts of details about warehouses, delivery van computer systems, and the other "behind the scenes" parts of your business.)

- **Management:** This section of the plan tells all about your management team members. Flaunts their backgrounds, their strengths, and the reasons why this is the right team to lead the company to marketplace success.

- **Key Competencies and Challenges**: This lays bare the strengths and weaknesses of your business, and uses both to define the peculiar competitive advantages you have in the marketplace.

- **Financials:** This is the section of numbers; at minimum, a balance sheet, a profit and loss statement, and both historical and projecting forward three to five years. Your particular plan can contain more or fewer or different sections than presented here, but it should hold the same information because that's what investors and lenders are looking for.

Who Writes the Business Plan?

The unique structure of your organization is what decides how you take on the process of creating your business plan.

If your organization is just you, then you get to write the plan. (Though you may want to invite a consultant to help you with some of the work.)

If your company is small and with a thin management layer, you probably still have to carry the most of the burden of creating your business plan. However, you can always offload some of the details to other members of the management team. If you operate a large company, you probably have a dedicated staff member or department for strategic planning or business development. Use this resource but still try a way to play a part in every step of the process. You can't afford to rely entirely on someone else for a plan that is yours.

The Essential Processes Involved

Whichever way you decide to proceed, the following are some definite steps you may need to take to craft that winning business plan:

- ✓ **Develop your strategy:** You need to have a business strategy to write a strategic plan. Use this phase to develop, fine-tune, or articulate your company's long-term strategy.

- ✓ **Gather the facts:** You need to assemble all manner of market facts and figures before you pen down a word in your plan, including information about your competitors. A business plan has to be built on a bedrock of reliable information.

- ✓ **Assemble the financials:** Not only do you have to assemble past and present financials, but you also need to make a three to five years growth plan of your business over the next. These numbers here required, don't come out of thin air, of course; there must be a reasonable basis for your well-analyzed projections, as well as a sales aspect to appeal to the potential investors.

✓ **Write the plan:** Once all your homework is done, it's time to do the actual writing. You can do this yourself if you're a good writer, or hire a professional, marketing-oriented writer to be on the safer side.

✓ **Format the plan:** You want your business plan to look as professional as possible. In that case, you may want to contract with an individual who has publishing experience to format your plan. Page layout, paper choice, number of colours, and use of graphics will all be decided at this stage.

✓ **Print the plan:** Find an excellent printer and print the plan. Enough said.

✓ **Use/Present the plan:** When you get to the point of presenting your plan to potential lenders and investors, you might find that creating the business plan was the easy part. This part can involve anything from a simple one-on-one discussion to an insanely intricate show complete with a multimedia PowerPoint presentation.

Analyze Your Audience

Creating a plan without a target audience in mind is the biggest mistake to make when creating a business plan. Without a purpose or a defined goal; you may follow all the steps and observe all the rules, but end up creating something generic.

It is much better to know beforehand who will be reading your plan and why; so, you can craft your plan to appeal to that particular audience. You also get to know what you can leave out when you know who your target audience is, (because they either know it already or don't care about it) and what you should shine more light on (because they either expect to see it or are particularly interested in it). When you know your audience, you know whether your plan should be short or long, simple or complex, and plain or fancy.

Determining Your Audience

All this talk about creating the type of business plan that best suits your audience hinges on one question: *Who is your audience?*

There are possibly three potential audiences for your business plan:

- Potential lenders and investors

- Your customers

- Your employees

Common sense leads us to conclude that, although some of your customers might want to know your company's business plan, most customers are more interested in the products and services you're selling, and more concerned with the prices you're charging. In short, your creating a business plan does not benefit your customers.

Creating a business plan that provides clear strategic guidance for your employees, mainly your key managers, is a noble idea, defeated only by the fact that most of internal business plans end up sitting on a shelf collecting dust. In as much as your business needs a strategic direction which a good business plan can provide, you're likely not going to go to all the trouble to create a business plan purely for in-house purposes.

Having done the elimination, you're left with one target audience; the people that you'd like to lend you money. Depending on your particular business and its financing needs, this audience of lenders and investors can consist of several different types of entities:

- **Bankers and loan officers:** You'd typically go to a bank or a lending firm for a loan, if your capital needs are small, or if you want to maintain complete control over your business.

- **Venture capitalists:** Venture capital firms are companies that specialize in investing both money and their expertise in startup businesses, in return for a significant equity position in the company. Most often, venture capitals expect relatively high rates of return on their investments.

- **Strategic investors:** These are typically large companies that invest more substantial sums often over $1 million for a larger equity stake in your company in return.

- **Small investors:** Small investors, typically referred to as "friends and family," are individuals who lend relatively tiny sums of money in exchange for an appropriate ownership stake in your company.

Writing for Your Audience

Although each of these different audiences possesses its unique wants and needs, they all have one thing in common: They're in the business of handing out money, and you sure want some of it.

Each of these target audiences expects that a business plan will present the information and strategy that will convince them that your business is either a good investment or a reasonable loan risk. They expect your plan to be in a specific format, to contain accurate data, and to somewhat resemble other similar plans from other businesses in your market niche. They expect you to follow an outline in which everything is in the right place and format so that they can easily find the information that is important to them.

This may sound a little restrictive, but it makes your job easier. It's just like it is in the day-to-day running of your business. When you know what your customer wants, you know what kind of product you have to deliver.

What happens, you may ask, if you don't write your business plan for a specific audience? In the worst of all possible scenarios, if you don't give the audience what it expects (in terms of content and format), it might cause them to simply toss your plan aside without even a cursory read. That outcome is not only possible; but it is also likely, especially if a lender or investor has dozens of other similar proposals on his or her desk at the same time. These people are looking for a reason; any reason to whittle down the stack of proposals by rejecting unworthy candidates. Making the first cut is essential, and any deviation from standard operating procedure marks your business plan for the outbox.

You Are Not the Audience

The first thing to keep in mind when writing for your audience is that you're not writing for yourself, or your staff or advisors or friends or family. It doesn't matter what you'd wish to see included in the business plan; if your audience doesn't have interest in it, you shouldn't feature it.

The opposite is also true, of course. There may be information that you simply feel is irrelevant, shared knowledge, or (more likely) boring. Your feelings, in this case, don't matter. If the audience expects to or needs to see this information, it should go in the plan. No questions asked.

Remember, you're writing for your audience (your banker, the VC firm, etc) and not for anyone else. Your audience can be one person (in the case of your banker), or it could be many different persons or groups of people. It doesn't matter. What they're all interested in is to see is what goes into the plan. Nothing more, nothing less.

It's important to notice that your audience probably may not know as much about your business as you do. You may need to include some fundamental information about your market, the type of business you're in, and the like, just to bring your audience up to speed. Don't assume that your audience knows very much about your business. Unless, based on similar investments or experience, you're sure they do.

For the same reason, you would want to avoid using buzzwords and acronyms that are foreign to the uninitiated. If you're in the cellular phone industry, you're familiar with terms like CDMA and TDMA and GSM; your potential investors probably aren't. (Unless, they're VCs who have invested in other cellular firms.) If you can't avoid the buzzwords, as some of them can't be avoided; you should take the time to define and explain them on first use.

Your Audience Is the Audience

The only audience you should be writing for; the only people with opinions that really count are the people and firms that you want to inject money into your business. Your goal in producing this plan is to entice these entities to make a loan or an investment. Everything in your business plan; every tiny section, every graphic, every word, should be targeted at this audience and should be geared towards accomplishing your goal.

The better you know your audience, the better you can aim your business plan to hit their "Yes Button." If your audience is a single individual (the loan officer at your bank, for example, or a particular partner at a VC firm), write your plan for that individual. Don't even pretend to create a plan with a global application; make sure every page of your plan is meaningful to your target individual.

If your audience is multiple individuals or a combination of multiple types of individuals, your job becomes slightly more complex. It's possible that you're presenting your plan to two different banks or two different VC firms, each of which has somewhat different hot buttons. That's a more onerous task but not an impossible one. Remember, they're both investors (or lenders), and similar factors drive both.

Your task only becomes herculean when you try to target your business plan to convince two entirely different constituencies. For example, if you expect your plan to appeal to both investors and employees, you're simply trying to ensnare yourself. You will end up compromising your success with at least either of the two constituencies; if not both of them! In this example, you're likely not to get the investment you want and alienate your employees, all in one fell swoop.

If you must distribute your business plan to two different audiences, consider creating two different business plans. This isn't an accounting-type situation, where creating two sets of books will buy you trouble with the Feds. It's perfectly acceptable and particularly recommended to write two different audience-specific business plans, one to spur investment and the other as a guide to your employees.

To this end, it's a shame that the business plan you share with potential investors is called a "business plan." If this document were subject to truth-in-labelling laws, it would be called an "investor enticement plan". The fact that it's referred to as a business plan, which is commonly understood to be a type of internal strategic plan is misleading, particularly to those charged with creating the document.

Understanding Specific Audiences

When writing your plan, you need to understand what your specific audience expects to see. What drives your audience—what information do they need before they can say "yes" and write you a check?

Let's take a look at the four different types of potential lenders and/or investors and how you can fine-tune your plan for most excellent appeal.

What the Audience Would Want to Know

The driving force behind a yes or no decision by an investor is how he or she assesses the risk, which is also a factor of how you present it; that is, how likely is it that you will not be able to repay the loan? Again, lenders are not very interested in getting a return on their investment. They more concerned about their loan getting repaid (plus interest, of course). To that end, how fast and how far you can grow your business is likely not as relevant to a lender as it is to an investor; more interest is in the stability of your business and your ability to generate sufficient cash flow over the loan period to pay back.

Here is a checklist of the types of things you would want to include in any business plan targeted at loan officers, bankers, and other lenders

- ✓ Historical cash flow statement

- ✓ Historical balance sheet

- ✓ Historical profit and loss statement

- ✓ Projected cash flow statement

- ✓ Projected balance sheet

- ✓ Projected profit and loss statement

- ✓ Successful prior experience in management bios

- ✓ Detailed information about the market potential

- ✓ Evidence of stability (market stability, business stability, management stability)

- ✓ A detailed plan of how the loan will be used

Analyze Your Market

As you will learn later in this book, a good business plan tells a story; and the first part of the story defines why you want to pursue this particular business opportunity. The reason why has to do with the revenue and profit potential represented by a specific market. There's an attractive market opportunity, and this business plan describes how we're going to get our share of that opportunity.

To drive a point with your market potential, you would need to tell your potential investors about the market, what it is all about, how big it is, the major players already in it, and how it's going to grow. However, to deliver this information with any degree of authority, you have to become very familiar with the dynamics of your particular market.

Understanding your market is a business requirement that, unfortunately, many business owners take too lightly. It's very easy to get lost in the day-to-day operations of your business, get sucked into the high-profile world of conferences and high finance, or carried away in "inside" thinking of your product development team and thus lose track of the customers and the market that drive your business. Staying in touch with your customers is hard work, but if it's not working you can neglect or delegate.

Why Market Analysis Is Important

You running your business is already a full-time job. Why do you have to invest time digging up information on what other companies are doing? How could the activities your competitors possibly affect what your company does?

The reality is that market research and analysis is vital to the success of any business; its importance to the creation of a successful business plan only highlights that overall significance.

The Market Drives Everything

Why should you have a consistent focus on market research and analysis? There are several important reasons.

First, let's not overlook the obvious. As discussed in the previous chapter, there are certain types of information that potential lenders and investors expect to see in your business plan. One of these items is a section on your market; how big it is, who plays in it, how it's going to grow, and so on. So, at the very least, you need to engage in some basic market research and analysis to create this section of your business plan.

Second, and more importantly, the more informed about your market, the better you can focus your business, your products, and your services. The "Market," after all, is just another word for the whole universe of potential customers for your business. Knowing your market means knowing your customers, and every businessperson worth his or her salt knows that understanding your customers is the single most crucial factor in business success.

Some would go so far as to say that knowing the market is, or, to say the least, should be second nature to every successful business owner. Truly market-focused businesspeople live and breathe the market; they know their customers' needs and whims, they know the fads and trends, they know what's happening in each distribution channel, they even know what their competitors are up-to before it happens. To a successful businessperson, the market is his or her life.

That's because everything you do is to serve the market. If you lose touch with the market, then your business is also out-of-touch, and an out-of-touch business quickly becomes a failing business.

That is the reason knowing your market is very vital to the success of your business. It's not just for the business plan; knowing your market helps you to create a long-term strategy that drives your company's current and future actions.

Defining Your Market

A market is typically defined by the goods and services it offers and by the types of customers that exist for those goods and services.

If you're not sure of what to call your market, look to your industry's trade publication and research reports. It's likely, the press and the analysts have a phrase for the business space where you play; if so, take a clue from it.

Your Competitors' Market Is Your Market

If you're still unsure precisely what market it is that you play in, take a look at your direct competitors. If your competitors are focused, that focus of theirs will likely describe the same market you're targeting. You can describe your market, then, by the customers, your competitors target and by the types of products and services that they offer.

However, know that defining a market from your competitors' game-plan is not the same as defining a market by your competitors. A market is defined by its products and customers, not by the companies that compete in the market. (It's not the Toshiba and IBM market; it's the portable computer market.) So, be mindful to avoid a competitor-focused description of your market.

Broad or Narrow?

A market can as much be defined broadly or narrowly. You may want to set distinct market features that best suit the specific products and services that your company offers.

For example, defining a market as the "communications market" is relatively broad and includes all sorts of communications products and services; everything from cellular telephone networks and landline phone services to cordless telephone handsets and walkie-talkies. A narrower definition would be the market for "mobile communications devices," which would cut exclude all the networks and services (along with all desktop phone products) to focus specifically on mobile phones and walkie-talkies.

Obviously, the broadest market definitions would describe the largest revenue opportunities, along with the most significant number of competitors. It's easy to get lost in this type of market definition; you become a tiny fish in a massive pond, and it will look like you're competing with a number of established industry behemoths.

The narrowest market definitions, on the other hand, run the risk of describing minimal (and potentially uninteresting to investors, at least) revenue opportunities. If you define your market too narrowly, you may put yourself in a corner; future growth may depend on expansion in a direction that appears to exceed the restrictive bounds you've described for your market.

Quantifying Your Market

Once you've defined your market, you need to size it. What is the size of the current market? Forecasting market size in the present and the future will help to identify the potentiality of the market to decide whether to venture into the market or not and to project the obtainable sales volume for the target market. Suffice to say that it is so possible that the product that you are thinking of bringing to the market is a matured product in that many people already are providing such products. If this is the case, the question you should ask yourself is: What makes you different? Does the market still have ample capacity to absorb this product? Would they be people within the target market that would still be able to accommodate whatever it is that we bring in, and also provide the necessary level of patronage for your products?

Another set of questions to ask: What is the size of the total market? Can this overall market be grown, or is it something that is finite and cannot be expanded?

For us to be able to determine the target sales volume, would multiply the market size with the target market share for.

Example, if the total market size is one million persons and we have targeted to serve just 25% of the market. What that means is that our sales revenue can only be based on 250,000 people which represent a target market share of 25%.

Target sales volume = market size × target market share

Markets are built to grow or shrink. So, the question is. How do we exterminate market growth? There are two considerations that we look at when we look at market growth.

- **Historical growth:** The first consideration is how has the market grown in the past; usually, this is expressed in terms of percentages. How much percentage represents the growth in the market over the years?

- **Environmental factors:** Another thing that influences market growth is environmental factors and are explained below:

1. Economy, especially if it's a consumer product. The more disposable income within the economy, the higher the probability of growth for most consumer products.

2. Technology, in the last few years several developments in the technological terrain have changed the taste and how people want to access the market, so we need to consider that when are estimating market growth

3. Legal factors, that's the law and regulations also affect market growth.

4. Substitute or alternative products.

Detailing the Market

Sizing your market is part of the equation. The other part is describing your market, how it's built and how it works.

There are several components of a comprehensive market description:

- **Products and services:** For your business plan, you'll need to describe the types of products and services offered within your industry.

- **Customers:** You'll probably need to describe the types of customers your industry targets (consumers, corporations, and so on), the demographics of these customers (men between 25 and 45 with incomes above $100,000, for example), and if a few major customers represent a large per cent of sales—the names of the industry's key customers. (This last point would be more suited if you're a manufacturer selling to wholesalers or retailers, your largest customers would be the major distributors and retailers who stock and sell your product.)

- **Competitors:** What are the biggest companies in your industry? What are their estimated revenues? (You might be left with guessing at this.) What are their individual market shares? What are their unique strengths and weaknesses? Are they gaining or losing ground in the marketplace? To be equipped for effective competition, you need to know as much about your competitors as possible.

- **Distribution channels:** Do you sell directly to consumers, do you sell to retailers (two-step distribution), or do you sell through wholesalers that then sell to retailers (three-step distribution)? Or do you sell via mail order, direct mail, telemarketing, a Web site, or through a dedicated sales force or third-party sales reps? However things get sold in your industry, it needs to be described.

- **Promotional activities:** How do companies in your industry promote their products and services to prospective customers? Do the companies run adverts and, if yes, where and to what degree? In which ever way your industry supports its sales needs to be described.

- **Average margins:** How much profit does the typical company in your sector generate, as a per cent of sales? Knowing an average industry profit margin will help you better build your financials and will lend an air of credibility to the financial projections you make to potential investors.

- **Other analytics:** If you have the numbers, there are several other interesting data points you can calculate. These analytics can be useful for making comparisons between your company's performance and industry averages: sales per employee, profit per employee, advertising as a per cent of revenues, development cost as a per cent of revenues, and so on.

The important thing is that you need to know how your market ticks, even if you don't have precise numbers not just to create your business plan but, more importantly, to help you develop your overall business strategy. You can't figure out how to get from point A to point B unless you know the landscape!

Analyze Your Strengths

As you develop your company's long-term business strategy—and prepare to mould that strategy into a business plan—not only do you need to know your customers and your competitors (as discussed previously), you need to know your company. You need to understand what your company does, of course (what products and services you sell and to whom), but you also need to know all about your strong points and your weak points.

You can be sure that your competitors know your strengths and (especially) your weaknesses and are right now plotting how to defend against your strengths and target your weaknesses for offensive action. If you're up on your market, you're doing the same for your competitors.

If your competitors can (and do) identify your strengths and weaknesses, so can (and should) you.

Once you have this information in hand, you can develop a strategy to build on your strengths and strengthen your weaknesses —both of which are essential for long-term success.

There's another reason for identifying your strengths and weaknesses—you'll need this information for your business plan. Most business plans include a section called Competitive Advantages (or Core Competencies or something similar) that details your company's strengths; most plans also include a section called Competitive Challenges (or Potential Liabilities or the like) that details your weaknesses. So you'll need to have a handle on your strengths and weaknesses before you start writing your business plan.

Identifying What You Do Well

The things you do well are your strengths or your core competencies. The things you do uniquely well, or demonstrably better than your competitors, become unique competitive advantages.

It's important to differentiate between common strengths and unique strengths. A common strength is something you're inherently good at; a unique strength is something you're better at than your competitors.

In the course of defining your company's strengths and weaknesses, you should count your common strengths and your unique strengths as two separate items. This is because one of your common strengths may also be a strength for one or more competitors, whereas a unique strength is something your company alone possesses. A unique strength can be turned into a competitive advantage; if you can do something, your competitors can't, that gives you some degree of advantage in the marketplace. And, as you know, you'll take every marketplace advantage you can get.

Different Kinds of Strengths

What types of activities represent strengths? Although there are hundreds of different areas in which your company can excel, you can group those activities into five primary types:

- Product strengths

- Brand strengths

- Marketing and advertising strengths

- Sales and distribution strengths

- Operational strengths

Product Strengths

Product strength is one of the most important strengths to attain because your customers directly see it, and should directly impact your sales. There are many ways to establish a product strength: Your product can be of higher quality than the competition; it can be available in a wider variety of outlets and channels; it can be available in a wider selection of colours or sizes or options; it can be lower priced than the competition; it can have a better reputation than the competition. The key is that the strength is directly attributable to the product.

Brand Strengths

Brand strength is similar to product strength, but the quality is held by the overall brand rather than the individual product. Individual products sold under that brand often (but not always) share the brand strengths by association. A brand might be known for quality, price, innovation, fun, status, or lots of things.

Marketing and Advertising Strengths

Some companies know how to market their products and services; others don't. Great marketing or advertising campaign will increase awareness of your product and (in some cases) your company; greater awareness should, at least in theory, lead to higher sales.

Sales and Distribution Strengths

If your sales force can get more items stocked than your competitors' sales forces can, then you've just identified a sales/distribution strength. If your sales force can push your product into more channels than your competitors can, that's another sales/distribution strength. The ability to get your product stocked or, in the case of direct-sales models, to make a sale directly to the end customers is a necessity; if you can do it better than your competitors, it's a strength.

Operational Strengths

Operational strengths relate to processes that occur behind the scenes. You may be able to ship your products faster than your competitors; that's an operational strength. You may be able to produce your product at a lower cost; that's an operational strength (that can also translate into a product strength— lower prices). If you have a more efficient warehouse operation, that's an operational strength.

Other Strengths

There are many other types of strengths that your company could possess. Your firm could have a strategic vision that always gets you to new opportunities sooner than your competitors; in this instance, your strategy is your strength. Your firm could be so well known in your industry that you're always getting

interviewed by the trade and consumer press;
in this case, your public awareness is a strength.

Determining Your Strengths

How do you know when your company has a bona
fide strength and, not just something you think you do
well?

The first thing to do is look at everything your
company does, all its processes and activities, from top
to bottom. Note which activities appear to be running
smoothly and which appear to have some rough
edges. Focus on the smooth-running operations, and
you've made your first cut.

Next, look at each of those smooth-running
operations and ask yourself what impact each one has
on your revenues and profits. (Remember that an
activity that reduces costs increases profits.) Rank

these operations by their monetary impact and get ready for the next step.

Now, in order of importance, start comparing your best operations to those of your competitors. If you think you have a particularly impactive sales force, compare your sales force's results to those of your chief competitors. If you believe you get products to market extremely fast, compare your time-to-market with that of your competitors. If you feel your product is of higher quality, test it. Do whatever you need to do to prove (to yourself, if to no one else) that you are doing this one thing better than anyone else in your industry.

Learning from Your Strengths

Once you've found a bona fide competitive advantage, tear it apart. Look at that advantage from every angle. Figure out why it exists and what your company has done to create that advantage. Answer the question, "Why is this thing so good?"

If you don't examine your strengths, you'll never be able to replicate them. The goal is to determine what you've done right so you can do something similar elsewhere in your organization.

A related goal is to preserve your strengths. Again, if you don't know how the strength came about, if you don't know what you're doing right, then you probably won't know how to keep doing it right. Analyze your strengths just as a competitor would; when you understand what you're good at, you'll get even better.

Finally, you need to exploit your strengths. If you can ship products to customers one day faster than any of your competitors, then make that one day a big issue. Play up not only how quickly you ship but also how your customers benefit by getting your product one day sooner. Turn your company's strength into a consumer benefit, and you'll get the full benefit of your competitive advantage.

Figuring Out Where You're Weak

Just as your company has its strengths, it also has its weaknesses. For everything you do well, you probably do an equal number of things not so well. It's a fact of life; no one's perfect!

Determining your company's soft underbelly is of equal importance to determine your strengths, and may be more important over the long run. When you discover a weakness, you now have a project, to either mitigate or improve the thing that is weak. The more weaknesses you can eliminate, the more stable your company will be.

Understanding Different Kinds of Weaknesses

Any area that can be a strength can also be a weakness. Some areas are more critical than others; a rotten product will ultimately derail even the best sales force or advertising campaign. Here, then, are the key areas in which to look for inherent weaknesses:

- **Product weaknesses:** Product quality is probably the biggest killer. If your product or service doesn't deliver as promised, everything else you do will also suffer. You have to ensure that your product is at least as good as your competitors' products, just to stay in the game.

Product quality isn't the only possible product weakness, however. Your product can be too pricey or not expensive enough. (Too low a price can sometimes convey poor quality.) Your product might not be available in the right colours or sizes or other variations, it might not be available in as many different outlets, or it may be outdated. (Last year's product available this year is of little use.) Worst of all, your product might simply not be available at all; if your competitors beat you to market with the latest thing, that is a huge product weakness.

- **Brand weaknesses:** Just as you can have influential brand names, you can also have weak brand names. When it comes to quality and reliability, do you want to be known as the Volvo of your industry or the Pinto? Pinto is an equally recognizable brand, but it's a brand with a bad reputation. Given the choice of having a bad brand image or no brand image at all, you might want to choose the no-image option.

This leads into the other, a more common type of brand weakness is the lack of brand recognition. If your primary competitor has a recognized brand and you don't, you have a brand weakness problem. It doesn't matter how good your product is; if customers flock to a competitor's product because of its brand image, you're out in the cold.

- **Marketing and advertising weaknesses:** There are two major types of marketing/advertising weaknesses: bad marketing and no marketing. With the first type, it doesn't matter how big your budget is if your ads are ineffective. With the second type, it doesn't matter how effective your ads are if no one (or not enough people) sees them. You have to know what you're doing, and you have to spend the money to do it. Anything less—especially if your competitors are always out there in front of customers—is a competitive weakness.

- **Sales and distribution weaknesses:** If your competitors consistently achieve better stocking than you do, you have a sales weakness. If your competitors are in more and different outlets and channels than you are, you have a distribution weakness. It doesn't matter how good your product is or how effective your advertising is; if your product isn't on the shelves, nobody can buy it.

You face similar issues whether you're a retailer or you sell directly to your customers. If your customers can find the products they want—or if they're thwarted in their attempts to purchase those products— you'll lose those sales. Anything that stands in the way of your customer and the sale is a sales weakness that must be overcome.

- **Operational weaknesses:** Operational weaknesses too often sabotage the best business ideas. Maybe you have an excellent idea for a new product; if you can't get it built on time or at the right cost, you have a big problem. If orders or restocks sit in your warehouse for days and weeks without being fulfilled, you have a problem. If your systems are so poor that you end up with twice as much inventory as your competitors, you have a problem.

- **Other weaknesses:** Many other types of weaknesses could plague your company. If you have poor relationships with your employees— or if you don't pay them enough—you could have trouble holding on to experienced staff, with its resultant ill effects. If nobody in the industry (including your key suppliers) returns your phone calls, that's a weakness. If you're constantly playing catch-up because you're not savvy to market trends and developments, that's a weakness. If your company has a bad reputation in the industry (whether it's earned or not), that's a weakness that you have to work hard to overcome every day.

Cast a critical eye at everything your company does on a day-to-day basis. Anything you do poorly, or anything you don't do as well as your competitors, is a potentially devastating weakness.

Determining Your Weaknesses

You determine your weaknesses in the same way that you determine your strengths. Start by examining all of your company's processes and activities, as well as its image in the community, the workplace, and the marketplace. Note the negatives you find and isolate them for further examination.

Now, look at the activities that appear to be positives. These activities might be running smoothly in your eyes but might not be as efficient or as effective as similar activities from your competitors. If you find that your competitors are doing something better than you are, no matter how well you think you're doing it, that activity becomes a competitive weakness.

Once you've assembled this list of weaknesses; you can call them "things to improve" if you want, you need to rank the list by importance. Put the items that most put your business at risk at the top of the list and toss the minor annoyances to the bottom. Now you know what you need to attack.

Fixing What's Wrong—Or Minimizing Its Impact

Some things that are broken can be fixed. Some things that are weak can be strengthened. Some things that you're number two in can be improved so that you become number one.

Some things that are broken can't be fixed. Some things that are weak can't be strengthened. And some things can't be improved, no matter how hard you try. This means you might never be number one in that area.

One of the key skills of successful businesspeople is knowing which issues are worth spending their time on and which to let go of. Maybe you're stuck with an old, inefficient warehouse that would cost too much money to bring up to snuff. Perhaps you have a brand that was tarnished by some unspeakable event in the past. Perhaps your management team is so young it lacks necessary experience in your particular market.

If you can't fix something, learn to live with it. Perhaps you can compensate for the weakness by exploiting your strengths in other areas. Perhaps the area you're weak in isn't vital to your ultimate success. Perhaps you just have to drop back ten and punt. (Remember that a strategic retreat is still a viable strategy.)

If you have an inefficient warehouse, maybe you can speed up other parts of your operation—such as your product development or your shipping—to compensate. If you have a terrible brand, maybe you should just kill it or let it die a natural death. If you have an inexperienced management team, perhaps that means they can think outside the box and come up with new ways of doing old things.

Whatever your particular case, you need to recognize your weaknesses—and then incorporate those weaknesses into your overall strategy. Your strategy might be to fix the weaknesses, live with them, or cut your losses—but whatever you come up with, your response has to be strategic.

You can bet that your competitors are strategizing about how to exploit your weaknesses. It behoves you to strategize from the other direction and cut them off at the pass.

Analyze Your Strategy

A well-written business plans set down, in ink and paper, your business's long-term strategy. That alone is reason enough to develop a strategy before you start writing your business plan.

More important, however, is the fact that a business without a strategy is a business without direction or purpose. If all you do is come into the office at nine in the morning, make gas masks all day long, and then leave at five, you're not really going anywhere. You're just making gas masks.

If, on the other hand, you know you want to reach a certain revenue number in three years and to do that you have to make a certain quantity of gas masks each day, and they have to be of a certain quality and at a certain cost, then you have a purpose for everything you do. Yes, you'll still leave at five and come in at nine and make of gas masks in between, but now you'll know why and how you fiddle with the gas masks, and you'll certainly be able to incorporate new methods and processes to catapult you to that level you need to get.

What you are and what you want to be: There is a hierarchy of direction that drives every business. This direction starts with an overriding vision and filters down to specific tactics in the following manner:

- **Vision:** The dictionary definition of this word is "a mental image or imaginative contemplation." Applied to the business world, the vision is the reason you're in business; it's what drives your company and everything your company does. Even though visions should be unquantifiable and ultimately unachievable, organizations without a driving vision quickly loses guidance and becomes unfocused. It's the vision that steers your ship; without a vision, your business isn't going anywhere intended.

- **Mission:** The mission is the overall purpose of your business, more specific than your vision but not necessarily quantifiable. Missions are often presented in the form of a mission statement, which is a short, concise, often single-sentence statement of what your business is trying to achieve.

- **Goal:** A goal is an end or objective, specific to your mission, that your company strives to attain. Unlike your vision and mission, your goals are quantifiable.

- **Strategy:** Your strategy is your plan of action, designed to achieve your business goals. In other words, strategies describe how to meet your set goals and objectives.

- **Tactics:** A tactic is a method used to implement your strategy. Tactics, in a sense, are the details of your broader strategy.

Everything starts with the vision you have for your business. The vision is then translated into a specific mission, that is measured by one or more specific objectives. These goals are met by implementing an overall strategy, which is executed through individual tactics.

Here is a good example of how these five driving factors interact:

You might start by saying that the vision for your company is to be a global innovator in information technology. That's so vague to provide a general business direction, without being specific enough as to be limiting.

You can then say that the mission of your business is to solve the procurement problems of large, and medium-sized businesses. Again, this is unquantifiable, but it's also narrower in scope than the vision, and thus provides more specific direction.

Now you need to set a specific, quantifiable objective. You do this by stating that the goal of your business is to double its market share within five years. This goal is quantifiable and is a way of measuring how successful you are in pursuing your mission.

How do you achieve your goal? By stating that your strategy is to increase the value of your products while holding the line on pricing. Notice that no specifics were mentioned, even though you have set a general course of action.

Now it's down to the details. Your final statement is that your primary tactic within your strategy is to reduce manufacturing costs by sourcing critical components from overseas suppliers. When you put it correctly, the tactic is a marching order for the troops, specific step-by-step instruction for how to implement the strategy that achieves the goal that follows your vision and mission.

Vision

The vision you've got for your business defines what you are doing and the way you are doing. It sets the culture for your company and, when translated into a written statement, sets the entire tone for your business plan. In short, your vision describes your company and why it exists.

Your vision is the dream you've got, the reason you ventured into the business, the thing that drives you and all your employees. Everything you do in the business should be in the service of that dream, that vision.

Mission

Your mission is narrower than a vision but broader than a goal. Your mission is what you are driving your company to achieve, what you want it to become. Not in terms of achieving a particular revenue or profit number, but rather in terms of achieving something more general and less quantifiable.

A well-written mission statement, placed near the front of your business plan, defines the main target of your business. If you've got a vision of a world of peace and harmony, your mission can be to eliminate all hunger. (Your individual goals, then, might include reducing farm harvest loss in third world countries and introducing high yield crop variety to the sub Saharan Africa.)

Goals

Your goals are the primary quantifiable drivers you've got for your business. If your vision and mission direct you in the direction to head, your goals define precisely how far you want to get on that path and by when.

Goals also can measure how you're performing within the overall marketplace; they don't need to be entirely internal. Aiming at becoming the number two in the marketplace by year three is an example of an external goal, another one is the goal of attaining a 20 percent market share within a year.

Strategy

In business terms, your strategy defines how you've planned to achieve your financial and other goals. If your goal is to achieve a 20 per cent market share, your strategy can be to produce a better quality, lower-cost product than your competitors. (Your tactics would then describe precisely how you're going to lower costs and increase quality.) There are a lot of ways you could achieve your market-share goal; your strategy describes the one method you've chosen to take you there.

Tactics

Tactics are the day-to-day details of what your business is doing. They're low-level enough that they may not find their way into the business plan you present to potential investors; they're important enough, however, that they need to be communicated clearly to those employees who are charged with the execution of the plan.

Chapter Two

The Planning:

- ❖ Creating Your Outline
- ❖ The Narrative
- ❖ The Typical Elements
- ❖ Recommendations on the Length
- ❖ The Financials

Creating Your Outline

You may think that a business plan must be a complicated document, stuffed with complex sentences, overly technical terms, convoluted legalese, and detailed financial data. Nothing may well be farther from the reality. If you'll be able to talk about your business—and you no doubt can, at length—then you'll be able to create a good business plan.

The best business plans are conversational in tone, are easy to read and understand, avoid as much legalese as possible, and only include financial data that is necessary to paint an accurate picture of the business's potential. In fact, you could probably dictate the greater part of your business plan in a single setting, based on your inherent knowledge of what it is you're trying to accomplish and why.

The Narrative

Imagine you're sitting in a restaurant or a coffeehouse, and someone you know comes up and asks you what you're up to these days. You answer that you're in the process of starting up a new business, and then you start to tell a little story. You communicate to this person what your business is all about, why you've decided to get into this particular type of business, what kind of opportunity you see, and how you intend to exploit that opportunity. If you're on good terms with the person you're talking to; you might even share the revenues and profits you hope to generate.

Here's the type of story you tell:

Let me tell you about my business. We supply gas masks to hospitals and chemical plants across the United States, which is a pretty big market, and we hope to generate $12 million in revenues within the next three years.

I've always had this vision of every chemical plant staff and health worker in America using gas masks to improve the protection against occupational hazard. I've made it my mission to supply the market with the most extensive variety of high-quality gas masks available anywhere in the U.S. You see, every chemical factory and hospital should be providing gas masks to its workers, one per individual per quarterly. This creates a market for more than 15 million gas masks per year. At an average selling price of $20 per gas mask, that's a $300 million market, at retail.

I plan to create a line of gas masks that are customized for the protective gear market. Each gas mask will be available in the brand-conforming colors, as well as a variety of other fashionable colors and designs. I plan to hire a sales force to sell the gas masks to protective gear stores and then use strategic marketing to get the word out to the potential consumers.

I intend for my company to produce gas masks from a new factory we're building in Iowa. By utilizing this new, state-of-the-art facility, as well as labour from farmers working off-season, we can produce our gas masks for an average cost of about $5 per gas mask; which is about 10 per cent less than our competitors. We sell the gas masks to the protective gear stores at a 50 per cent discount, for an average net price of $10. That gives us a gross profit of $5 per gas mask.

Our organization will be lean and mean and be focused entirely on making and selling gas masks. All of our computer systems will have the latest gas mask-tracking software installed, and our new facility will have a special packing and shipping system designed especially for shipping gas masks. My senior management team is a mix of experienced gas mask makers and managers with experience in marketing products directly to CEOs and Directors of large firms.

Our real strength is our ability to produce gas masks in custom colors and designs and with a higher gross margin than our competitors. Now, I know we're new in the business, so we'll have to balance that with some splashy marketing and promotions. Still, I think we're coming with a lot of new ideas and better ways of doing things in the industry, and we'll be successful because of that.

I project that we can attain a 16 per cent market share by year three. In that year, we'll sell 2 million gas masks at an average net price of $10, which will generate $20 million in revenues. With our low-cost structure, I estimate that we'll operate on a 15 per cent net margin and generate $2 million of profits in our third year.

As you can see, this short story (of about 500 words) tells your audience members everything they need to know about your business. They know why you're starting the business, they see the opportunity presented, they understand how your company expects to profit from that opportunity, they sense the unique things that your company intends to do, and they learn how much money you expect to make if you follow your plan. It's all there, presented in a logical order; everything necessary is included, with nothing extraneous added.

The Elements of a Typical Business Plan

The way you tell your story about your business represents the basic framework on which you will build your business plan. Every major point in your story corresponds to a section in the plan; all you have to do is elaborate a bit on the crucial parts, and you'll have a comprehensive, well-organized business plan document.

The Basic Outline

There are many different patterns to organize the information in a business plan, but they pretty much conform to the following general outline:

✓ **Executive Summary:** This is a one-page overview of the major points in your plan, from your Vision and Mission all the way through your key financial goals. If your audience members just manage to read only this one page (which is all some will read), they'll absorb the relevant points of what your business is all about.

✓ **Vision and Mission:** Your Vision (sometimes called a Vision Statement) is a one-sentence statement of the dream you have for your business. Your Mission, otherwise called a Mission Statement, is a one-sentence statement of your business's main purpose. Some business plans do combine the Vision and Mission onto a single section and a single page; others may decide to separate them into different sections/pages for clarity.

✓ **Opportunity:** This section presents the market opportunity you've identified. Typically, this section starts by identifying the target market, sizing it, presenting growth opportunities, and discussing how other companies are pursuing this opportunity. This is where you utilize the market data and analysis you have gathered.

✓ **Market Strategy:** This section refers to the preceding section and describes how your company will pursue the identified opportunity. This section typically contains information about the products or services you'll be offering, and your sales, distribution, and marketing strategies for those products.

✓ **Business Strategy:** In this section, you finally get to talk in more depth about the business itself. You should present your business model and your revenue model. In other words, you communicate the reader how your business plans to make money.

✓ **Organization and Operations:** This is a detail-oriented section in which you describe (and show via an org chart) your company's structure, as well as the workings of key departments (manufacturing, warehousing, systems, and so on).

✓ **Management:** This section enables you to elaborate on (and brags a little about) your senior management team. You can also use this section to present members of your board of directors, and if appropriate, the key strategic and institutional investors.

✓ **Core Competencies and Challenges:** This section more or less sums up what's come before by listing your unique strengths and presenting potential challenges or weaknesses.

✓ **Financials:** This final section of your plan is where you put all relevant financial information, including profit/loss statements, balance sheets, multiyear revenue projections, and the like.

How Long Should It Stretch?

How big a business plan should you create? The proper answer is "as big as necessary", although that doesn't necessarily answer your question. The reality is that it's hard to do everything you need to do in fewer than 20 pages, and if you get much above 50 to 60 pages, your audience won't read it all. Aim for a middle ground in the 30-page range and realize that shorter is probably better.

How does this length break down by section? Here's a rough sketch of how you might organize a 30-page business plan; the TOC and any appendixes would be above and beyond this page count.

Recommended Page Count by Section

Section	# Pages
Executive Summary	1
Vision	1
Mission	1
Opportunity	4
Market Strategy	6
Business Strategy	6
Organization and Operation	6
Management	1
Core Competencies and Challenges	2
Financials	2
TOTAL	**30 Pages**

Adding Other Elements

This basic outline can, and should, at your discretion be augmented by several optional elements:

- **Cover page:** Your business plan needs to reflect the professional nature of your business, so spend some effort (or hire a graphic designer) to design a nice-looking cover page. Your cover should include your business's name and logo, the release date of the plan, and a title that reflects that this is a business plan.

- **Table of contents:** You need to provide an excellent roadmap to the various parts of the plan, in the form of a table of contents (TOC), which lists the page numbers of the major and minor headings in the plan.

- **Index:** If your plan is annoyingly long; more than 40 pages or so—readers will need a way to quickly reference items of interest. The best way to do this is through a detailed index.

- **Footnotes:** You don't have to embed all sorts of data and references in the body text of your plan; you can reference sources and other data through the use of nonintrusive footnotes and endnotes.

- **Appendixes and attachments:** Any information that needs to be included but doesn't fit within the main text, glossaries, press releases, and the like, can be added as an appendix or attachment.

What About the Financials?

Financial statements help you set the goals and measure the success of your business. They're an essential part of any business plan, and especially if you're borrowing money, they're every bit as important as any of the text sections.

Whether you're borrowing money or trying to attract investors, your potential lenders and investors will want to know what size business you're talking about, how profitable that business is, and how you expect to grow revenues and profits over the years. Your financial statements provide that critical information.

Although there are a few common financial statements that everyone will want to see, know that different lenders and investors will have different requirements in this regard; and various types of businesses will dictate different formats as well. You'll want to enlist the assistance of a qualified accountant or financial advisor to help you prepare these financial statements, and to prepare for any financial questions that may be asked of you.

A Quick Financial Refresher Course

Before we proceed to an examination of financial statements, let's brush up on some accounting basics.

Revenues, Expenses, And Profits

Three related concepts are key to the running of any business:

- **Revenues:** Revenues (also called sales) are the dollars you generate by selling your products and services. There are two types of revenues; gross revenues and net revenues. Gross revenues are the straight sales dollars you recorded; net revenues are your sales dollars less any returned or discounted sales. Revenues never have any costs or expenses deducted. It's pure sales; nothing else is included.

- **Expenses:** Expenses are your costs, the money you have to pay for various goods and services. There are several different types of expenses. Cost of goods sold (COGS) is product costs directly associated with the manufacture or purchase of the goods that contribute to your revenues. Operating expenses are those nonproduct costs that reflect the day-to-day operations of your business; salaries, rent, advertising, and so on. COGS and operating expenses are typically reported in different parts of your income statement.

- **Profits:** If revenues reflect how much money you take in and expenses reflect how much money you pay out, profits reflect how much money you have left after the two previous activities. (Profit is often referred to as income or earnings.)

Do not get these concepts confused. It's easy to slip and think of your revenues as "earnings" (since you "earned" that money!), but the word "earnings" actually refers to profits. Same with income; income is profit, not revenue. If in doubt, refer to the following table for some quick guidance:

Basic Financial Terms

Proper Names for What You Sell	What You Spend	What You Get to Keep
Revenues	Expenses	Profits
Sales	Costs	Earnings
		Income

Assets and Liabilities

Revenues, expenses, and profits are used to describe what your business does; assets and liabilities describe what your business owns and owes. Here's how they're defined:

- **Assets:** Assets are those items that your business owns. Assets can be in the form of tangible things (land, buildings, equipment, fixtures), cash or cash equivalents, or accounts receivable. In short, anything you own or that is owed to you is counted as an asset.

- **Liabilities:** Liabilities are the opposite of assets; they're things that someone else owns and for which you owe. Liabilities are typically in the form of loans, expenses, or taxes due.

If you take everything you own and subtract everything you owe, the balance represents your net worth in your business, also known as your equity. This equation is the core concept behind a balance sheet.

Equity Equation

Assets - Liabilities = Equity

Equity is the part of the business that is owned by its owners and investors, typically in the form of stock. Equity is calculated as assets less as liabilities.

The Difference Between Profits and Cash

You might think that the profits you make would feed the cash component of your assets. In theory, this could be the case; especially if you run a relatively small, relatively simple business. However, two factors can make these two numbers get out of whack.

First, you probably don't pay all your bills on the day you receive them. When a bill is due, but you haven't paid it yet, you have created a liability, which will change your asset position. Let's use an example in which you start with zero assets and zero liabilities. You sell a gas mask for $5 and, after subtracting $2 COGS, generate a $3 gross profit. That $3 in your pocket is both cash and asset, until you receive a sewer bill for $2. Now you have a $2 liability and a $2 expense. Even though you haven't paid the bill yet, you still have to figure the expense, which reduces your net profit to $1. You still have $3 in cash, but your profit is now just $1. So, for the time being, your cash doesn't equal your profit. (This will be rectified as soon as you write a check for $2 to the sewer commission, of course.)

The second way in which cash and profits differ is if you accept payment on credit. Let's say you sold that $5 gas mask (which generated a $3 gross profit) to Mr

Smith, who signed the invoice and promised to pay within 30 days. Now you have a $3 profit but zero dollars in cash, and you won't have the cash until Mr. Smith sends you a check later this month.

This is all to demonstrate why you must look at your cash situation as being separate from your company's profits, as tempting as it might be to think that your monthly profits would equate to real cash on hand.

Essential Financial Statements

There are many different ways to describe your business, but it's your financial statements that quantify your goals and performance.

There are dozens of different types of financial statements that you can use to describe your business. The three most common statements detail your firm's profits and losses (income statement), your firm's net worth (balance sheet), and your firm's cash on hand (cash flow projection). Other useful financial statements detail the sources of your revenues (revenue projection), project when your firm will start generating profits (breakeven analysis), and list all the "hard" assets that you own (capital asset inventory).

If you're unsure just which financial statements to include with your business plan, ask your audience; your potential lenders and investors typically have very precise requirements where financial information is concerned. Lacking any specific requests, three key types of financial statements probably should be included in every business plan. The following checklist details these essential financial reports:

Essential Financial Statements

- ✓ Income statements (current, historical, and a three-year or five-year projection)

- ✓ Balance sheet (current)

- ✓ Cash flow projection (monthly)

The Income Statement

The income statement reflects the revenue your company generates, the expenses you pay, and the profit (or loss) that filters down. The form of the income statement is to show your revenues, subtract the cost of goods sold to show the gross profit, and then subtract all your operating expenses to show your net profit. The series of equations look something like this:

Gross Profit Equation

Revenues - Cost of Goods Sold = Gross Profit

Net Profit Equation

Gross Profit - Operating Expenses = Net Profit

Your operating expenses are typically broken out into multiple line items. Also, you'll see the gross profit and net profit described as percentages of net revenues.

(When shown this way, they're called gross margin and net margin.)

The following figure presents the categories used in a typical income statement.

Here's a brief explanation of the most crucial income statement line items:

- **Gross Revenues:** This line (also called Gross Sales) reflects all of your dollar sales for the period, not counting any damaged or returned goods.

- **Returns:** Sometimes called "Returns and Allowances," this line reflects the cost of any returned or damaged merchandise as well as any allowances and markdowns.

- **Net Revenues:** Net Revenues (also called Net Sales) reflect your Gross Revenues less your Returns and Allowances.

- **Cost of Goods Sold:** This line (also called COGS or Cost of Sales) reflects the direct costs of the products you sold for the period.

- **Gross Profit:** This line reflects the direct profit you made from sales during this period. It is calculated by subtracting the Cost of Goods Sold from Net Revenues.

- **Gross Margin:** This line (also called Gross Profit Margin) describes your Gross Profit as a per cent of your Net Revenues. You calculate this number by dividing Gross Profit by Net Revenues.

- **Operating Expenses:** This line reflects all the indirect costs of your business. Typical line items within this overall category include Salaries, Advertising, Marketing, Selling, Research and Development.

- **EBITDA:** EBITDA stands for earnings before interest, taxes, depreciation, and amortization. Some people refer to this line simply as Net Income Before Taxes or Net Profit Before Taxes; the words "income," "earnings," and "profit" are synonymous. This line reflects the net profit your firm generated during the period, after all, actual costs have been accounted for but before you pay taxes and the interest on your loans and before you amortize or depreciate any capital assets. You calculate EBITDA by subtracting Operating Expenses from Gross Profit; a loss is notated within parentheses.

- **EBITDA Margin:** This line describes your EBITDA as a percentage of your Net Sales. You calculate this number by dividing EBITDA by Net Sales.

- **Net Profit (Loss):** This line (also called Net Earnings or Net Income) reflects your reported profit or loss after interest expenses, taxes, depreciation, and amortization costs have been factored out. You calculate this number by subtracting interest, taxes, depreciation, and amortization from EBITDA; a loss is noted within parentheses.

- **Net Margin:** This line describes your Net Profit as a percentage of your Net Sales. You calculate this number by dividing Net Profit by Net Sales.

You can present an income statement for a single period, or you can create an income statement that reflects a chronological impression. If you present an income statement for multiple periods (12 months, for example), you may want to include a final column that adds all the monthly numbers into a full-year number.

The Balance Sheet

The balance sheet is the financial statement that describes what your company owns (assets) and what it owes (liabilities). It's called a balance sheet because it, in effect, "balances" your assets and your liabilities in a variation of the previously presented equation.

Assets Equation

Liabilities + Equity = Assets

The assets go on the left side of the balance sheet, and the liabilities and assets go on the right; the bottom numbers on each side must be equal.

The following figure presents the categories used in a typical balance sheet.

- **Current Assets:** This category includes those items that can be converted into cash within the next 12 months. Typical line items would consist of Cash, Accounts Receivable, Inventories, and Short-Term Investments.

- **Fixed Assets:** This category (sometimes called Long-Term Assets) includes assets that are not easily converted into cash, including Land,

Buildings, Accumulated Depreciation (as a negative number), Improvements, Equipment, Furniture, and Vehicles.

- **Long-Term Investments:** This category includes any longer-term investments the company has made.

- **Total Assets:** This line reflects the value of everything your company owns. You calculate this number by adding together Current Assets and Fixed Assets.

The following are the key line items on the liabilities side of your balance sheet:

- **Current Liabilities:** This category includes any debts or monetary obligations payable within the next 12 months. Typical line items would include Accounts Payable, Notes Payable, Interest Payable, and Taxes Payable.

- **Long-Term Liabilities:** This category includes debts and obligations that are due to be paid over a period exceeding 12 months. Typical line items would include Long-Term Notes Payable and Deferred Taxes.

- **Equity:** This line (sometimes called Net Worth) reflects the owners' investment in the business. Depending on the type of ownership, this line may be broken into separate lines reflecting the individual equity positions of multiple partners or the company's capital stock and retained earnings.

- **Total Liabilities and Net Worth:** This line (sometimes called Total Liabilities and Equity) reflects the total amount of money due plus the owners' value. You calculate this number by adding together Current Liabilities, Long-term Liabilities, and Equity.

While an income statement can be looked at historically or projected into the future, a balance sheet is a snapshot of the present. It is not shown in any chronological progression.

The Cash Flow Projection

Your usable cash is not the same as the profits you generate. Potential lenders, especially, will want to know, on a month-by-month basis, whether you'll have enough cash on hand to pay the bills incurred during that period. You figure this out by generating a financial statement called a cash flow projection.

A cash flow projection might sound difficult and complex, but it's one of the easiest financial statements to create. You simply start each month with the amount of cash you have on hand, add the cash you expect to generate that month, and then subtract the cash you have to pay out. What you have left is your monthly cash position.

The equation to calculate your cash flow is as follows:

Cash Position Equation

Cash on Hand + Cash Receipts - Cash Paid Out = Cash Position

If your monthly cash position is positive, you have positive cash flow (meaning you paid all your bills and have some leftover); if this number is negative, you have negative cash flow (meaning you didn't have enough cash on hand to pay all your bills). Your cash position at the end of one month becomes your starting cash on hand for the next month; and you keep on like this, month-by-month, over the entire projected period.

Here's a brief explanation of the key line items in a cash flow projection:

- **Cash on Hand:** This is the amount of cash you have available at the start of each measurement period.

- **Cash Receipts:** These reflect the cash you generate throughout the measurement period.

- **Total Cash Available:** This is your initial cash on hand plus your cash receipts. It is the amount of money, in total, that you have available to pay out throughout the measurement period.

- **Cash Paid Out:** This reflects all the money you spend throughout the measurement period.

- **Cash Position:** This reflects your final end-of-period cash position. The amount of cash you project to have on hand at the end of the current measurement period. Your cash position at the end of one period turns into your Cash on Hand number at the beginning of the next period.

Margins and Ratios

The numbers contained in these financial statements paint a broad picture of your business. However, a more detailed understanding can be had by analyzing various combinations of numbers and comparing them to industry averages. How your business ranks in comparison will help potential lenders and investors determine how much of a risk your business represents.

Gross Margin

This number discussed previously, describes your gross profit as a per cent of net revenues. The equation is as follows:

Gross Margin Equation

Gross Profit ÷ Net Revenues = Gross Margin

This number in and of itself doesn't tell you much. Businesses in some industries operate on high gross margins because their cost of goods sold is meager. Businesses in other industries operate on low gross margins because the cost of products sold represents a high proportion of the final selling price. Saying that "XX per cent is the ideal gross margin" would be pointless.

However, comparing your business's gross margin to the gross margins of other similar businesses can be a useful exercise. If all your competitors operate at 50 per cent gross margin and you're squeaking along at the 40 per cent level, then something is obviously wrong. (Either your costs of goods sold is too high, or your selling prices are too low.) So this type of comparison is a viable analysis.

Also feasible is examining your company's gross margin over time. If over multiple periods, your gross margin shows a precipitous decline, that's a sign that something dramatic is changing in your business model. (Either your product costs are getting out of whack, or you're running too many sales, or you're offering too many discounts, or you're facing more aggressive competition; or something.)

Using your gross margin to provide comparative analysis, then, makes it a handy tool.

EBITDA Margin

EBITDA, as described earlier, is your profit before you have to extract the nebulous (and not always real) expenses of interest, taxes, depreciation, and amortization. Your EBITDA margin (sometimes called operating margin) is calculated by dividing EBITDA by net revenues, as in the following equation:

EBITDA Margin Equation

EBITDA ÷ Net Revenues = EBITDA Margin

You want your EBITDA margin to be a positive number; a negative EBITDA margin means that you're running an operating loss. Alas, as with your gross margin, the absolute number is next to useless. (Other than bigger is better, of course.) You need to compare your EBITDA margin with the EBITDA margin of similar businesses to determine whether you're reaching industry-average profitability. You can also analyze your EBITDA margin over time to detect any significant changes in the profitability of your business.

Net Margin

Net margin is similar to EBITDA margin, except it measures your profitability after interest, taxes, depreciation, and amortization have been subtracted.

You calculate net margin by dividing net profits by net revenues, like this:

Net Margin Equation

Net Profits ÷ Net Revenues = Net Margin

As with the EBITDA margin, the higher your net margin, the better. Especially when compared with similar businesses. A significant change in net margin over time reflects a change in the profitability of your business and bears examination.

Return on Investment (ROI)

All investors want to know what kind of return they're getting on their investments. There are actually two types of return on investment (ROI) equations that you can employ.

The first ROI equation describes the ROI of your business for a specific period and is based on current period net income and tangible net worth.

ROI Equation I

Net Income ÷ Tangible Net Worth = Return on Investment

The second ROI equation, shown next, measures the total return on a block investment.

ROI Equation II

Exit Value ÷ Initial Investment = Return on Investment

Obviously, you're always striving for a higher ROI, whichever valuation method you employ. When considering an investment, investors will estimate ROI and compare it against the ROIs represented by other investments. The investment with the higher potential ROI (and with an acceptable risk) will get the funding.

Current Ratio

Some lenders like to look at the liquidity of your business, as measured by the current ratio. You calculate your current ratio by dividing current assets by current liabilities, as shown in the following equation:

Current Ratio Equation

Current Assets ÷ Current Liabilities = Current Ratio

Liquidity is a reflection of how quickly you can convert assets to cash. Higher liquidity is desirable; having lots of cash on hand is better than having your cash tied up in assets that may or may not be able to be quickly converted into cash.

Quick Assets Ratio

Another way to evaluate liquidity is with the quick asset ratio. This ratio is similar to the current asset ratio, except it subtracts the cost of inventory from your existing assets; since inventory often cannot be liquidated quickly.

Quick Assets Ratio Equation

Current Assets - Inventory ÷ Current Liabilities = Quick Assets Ratio

Debt-To-Equity Ratio

The flip side of liquidity is debt. To evaluate a company's level of debt, you use the debt-to-equity ratio, shown in the following. If your debt-to-equity ratio gets too high, it's reflective of the business taking on too much debt.

Debt-To-Equity Ratio Equation

Liabilities ÷ Tangible Net Worth = Debt-To-Equity Ratio

Chapter Three

The Writing:

- ❖ Executive Summary
- ❖ Vision Statement
- ❖ Mission Statement
- ❖ Opportunity
- ❖ Data Presentation
- ❖ Market Strategy
- ❖ Business Strategy
- ❖ Organization and Operations
- ❖ The Outline

Executive Summary

The Executive Summary is a much-abbreviated version of your full business plan, located before the main body of your plan document. It should include most; but not all of the sections that comprise your plan, with each topic condensed to a paragraph or two.

The Executive Summary functions as a brief overview of your business plan. Someone reading only the Executive Summary should be able to get a general idea of what business you're in and why, as well as learn why your business is unique and how big it's going to get.

Even though the Executive Summary should only be a single page long, it's one of the hardest parts of the plan to write. Most business people find it easy to fill pages and pages with information about their business; condensing all that information to a single page is backbreaking work.

As Mark Twain once said, "I would have written a shorter letter, but I didn't have the time." The key to writing a successful Executive Summary is to know which information is indispensable and which isn't, and then to ruthlessly wield the red editing pencil to cut your plan down to its bare essentials.

If you do an excellent job on your Executive Summary, you'll have a single page that tells your entire story concisely and convincingly. If you do a terrible job of it, you'll end up with a multiple-page mess that does nothing more than duplicate similar information in the body of your plan.

When it comes to Executive Summaries, shorter is definitely better.

Why You Need an Executive Summary

First, as short as your business plan is; there are many people who won't read the whole thing. In the hectic world of your potential lenders and investors, the time it takes to read a full 20-page document might not always be available. Especially when a lender or investor is evaluating a large number of proposals, being able to spend five minutes vetting a summary is preferable to spending a half-hour or so reading the entire thing. If your plan is the one that doesn't include a summary, it might not get read at all.

The second reason to include an Executive Summary is that it helps set the stage for the rest of the document that follows. Think of it as a trailer for a motion picture or the back-cover blurb for the latest novel. The Executive Summary prepares the reader for the main document; and if worded properly, "teases" the reader in a way that whets his or her appetite for what follows.

A business plan without an Executive Summary is incomplete. Your readers will expect this overview, and they'll expect it to be exactly what its name suggests; a short (emphasis on the word short) summary of your plan, for busy executives.

What To Include In The Executive Summary:

When creating your Executive Summary, you have a single page to work with (see the following figures). What should go on that page?

Vision

> It's good to start your Executive Summary the same way you start the main part of your business plan, with a statement of why you're in this particular business. That means including your single-sentence vision statement, in most cases exactly as written in the Vision section of your plan.

Mission

> Next up is your mission statement, from the Mission section of your business plan. Assuming your mission statement has been held to a

single sentence, you can cut and paste this exactly as presented in the Mission section.

Opportunity

Now the editing begins. The next part of your Executive Summary should be a single paragraph describing the market opportunity offered to your business. This paragraph will summarize the key data presented in the Opportunity section of your plan.

You need to boil down the market information to the bare essentials necessary to paint a compelling picture of market opportunity. Include market size and growth, the number of potential customers (if available), and a basic explanation of why the market is sized or growing the way it is.

Market Strategy

Next up are one or two paragraphs that describe how your business is responding to this market opportunity. This part of the summary abridges the complete Market Summary section of your business plan, with an emphasis on the products and services you'll be offering.

This part of the Executive Summary will require extreme editing from the full Market Opportunity section of the business plan. You should only present information necessary to describe your business and products; you probably don't need to talk about competitors, advertising, packaging, distribution, and the like. Keep your focus on the products and services you'll be offering and leave the rest of the marketing and sales details to the Market Opportunity section.

Business Strategy

The business strategy part of your Executive Summary abridges the Business Strategy section of the main plan document. You should be able to present the key information in no more than two paragraphs.

Use this part of the summary to tell the reader about your business; what business you're in, what business model you employ, how you're going to generate revenues and profits, and what sets you apart from the competition. Do not include information about specific departments in your organization, and don't get too wrapped up in the details of what you do present.

The key to this short section is being able to convey your company's unique business proposition. Convey either directly or indirectly, the one important thing you do that gives you a leg up on competitors. Your unique business proposition should be the reason investors invest in your company rather than in a competitor; if they're sold on the market opportunity, they have to choose which firm to back, and each company's unique business proposition greatly influences that choice. Identify yours straight away in the Executive Summary and draw attention to it.

Financial Goals

Businesspeople are divided on the topic of what financial information to include in the Executive Summary. The numbers-oriented crowd (accountants, financial analysts, bankers, and so on) will argue that as complete a set of financials as possible should be included in the front of the plan. (This is most likely because this crowd is only interested in the numbers and will probably pass over the narrative part of the document to get right to the spreadsheets.) Other, more marketing-focused businesspeople will opt for including little or no financial information in the summary part. (This is most likely because this crowd believes that the real story is with the opportunity and the business; the numbers are secondary.) The right numbers to include probably fall between these two camps.

Despite the protestations of accountants everywhere, there is unlikely to be any real value in providing a full set of numbers on the Executive Summary page. Anyone who wants to see the full financials can quickly flip to the back of the plan to access the Financials section.

Vision and Mission

Every business starts with a vision and a mission. The vision describes how you see the world, and the mission describes your business purpose. Together, these two statements define why you're in business and what reason this particular business has to exist.

Your vision and mission are presented in the Vision and Mission sections of your business plan. Although these are the shortest sections of your plan (no more than a paragraph each), they may be among the most challenging parts to write. That's because many business people find it challenging to articulate the reasons why they do what they do.

"I just make gas masks," you might respond if asked why you're in business. But in reality, you make gas masks because you have some sort of vision for gas masks' role in the world at large, and you've set for yourself a mission to help achieve that vision.

It's getting to that core rationale; the overriding idea that drives everything you do. That is key to creating compelling vision and mission statements.

The Vision Statement

The vision statement you write for the business plan should express your ultimate dream for the market or consumers your company targets. You are guided by your dreams, and your company should be driven by your vision. Anyone reading the Vision section of your business plan should immediately know why you do what you do and should get a sense of what it is that your company is trying to accomplish.

In other words, the Vision section describes why your company exists; which is why it's the very first section (after the Executive Summary, of course) of your plan. An effective Vision section sets the tone for the entire business plan and provides a sense of purpose that has driven you to seek funding from the people reading the plan.

Criteria for An Effective Vision Statement

The Vision section of your plan should consist of a simple statement of vision, ideally no longer than a single sentence. (That's right; the entire section is just a sentence long!)

The vision statement should be a somewhat broad, somewhat vague declaration. Remember, your vision statement doesn't describe your mission (that's what the mission statement is for) or define your goals; your vision statement expresses your dreams.

The ideal vision statement should meet these criteria:

- It must be short, one sentence, ideally, and no more than a paragraph at the longest.

- It must be to the point; it shouldn't ramble.

- It must be focused on a single thought or topic.

- It must be sufficiently farsighted and "big" in concept as to be virtually unquantifiable.

- It must provide a distinct focus and direction for the business to follow.

The Mission Statement

Where your vision statement defines the why behind your business, your mission statement describes the what. What it is that your business does and what it is that you're trying to achieve.

The Mission section of your plan directly follows the Vision section and is also a single-sentence (or single-paragraph) section. It has a narrower focus than the Vision section and truly defines the type of business you're in. Someone reading your Mission section should know immediately what your company does, and what you don't do.

Opportunity

The Opportunity section of your plan (sometimes called Market Opportunity, Market Dynamics, or just The Market) is the first meaty section you need to prepare. This goal of this section is to describe the market opportunity you seek to pursue and convince potential investors that it's a significant enough opportunity to be worth pursuing.

As such, this section will include substantial narrative text (you have to tell a story about the market) and a large amount of numerical data. Which data you choose to present, how you want to present it, and how you weave it into your narrative will determine the effectiveness of this section.

When the Opportunity section is complete, you should have four pages or so of compelling market information. The reader should understand the fundamental nature of the market, the size of the market, the market's growth rate, the types of customers who comprise the market, and the key competitors in the market. Potential lenders and investors don't have to (and don't want to) absorb trivial details about how the market works. Still, they should be left with an excellent understanding of the issues that will drive your business decisions.

Writing the Opportunity Section

The Opportunity section of your plan needs to be about four pages long; less if your market is relatively small and easy to understand, more if it's a complex market with a lot of different submarkets. This section needs to not only describe the market but also layout the business opportunity that you want your company to pursue.

After you've gathered your market data, you need to create a detailed outline for the Opportunity section.

As you write the section, you'll need to "chunk" the text into easily digestible parts, each part with its heading (or subheading). The individual points in your outline should become your section heads and subheads.

As a general rule, you don't want to go more than four or five paragraphs without having a header of some sort. This helps the reader visually find key topics and enables you to create a very detailed table of contents based on the section heads and subheads.

How detailed should your outline be? Here's an example of a detailed Opportunity section outline for a business focusing on the mobile phone market:

The Opportunity section that follows this outline will be divided into four major sections: Wireless Market Size and Growth, Emerging Products and Services, Industry Trends, and Competitive Dynamics. Within each of these sections will be multiple subsections; for example, the Wireless Market Size and Growth section will contain two subheads. U.S. Market and Global Market. Some of these subheads will contain a half-page or more of information; others will only be a single paragraph long.

The key point is to outline your market logically and make the information flow to tell your story. You want to tell the reader what the industry is all about, how big it is, how much it's growing, and what new things are happening that make it even more attractive. You can also use this section to talk about key industry players, although that information can also go in the Market Strategy section. It's your call.

Different Formats for Data Presenting

As you tell the story of your market, there are several different ways to present your key points. Much of your information will be presented in narrative text, of course, but some key data will be numeric—market size, growth, the number of customers, and so on.

You can choose to present numeric data within the textual narrative, you can bullet the data, you can break it out into tables, or you can show it in a graph format. All four options have their advantages and disadvantages, and you may want to show some key pieces of information in multiple formats. For example, you may want to break out historical revenue data into a bar graph but then repeat the key data points in the text.

Bullets

If you're afraid of "burying" key data within a long text paragraph, considering breaking out the data into a bulleted list. As you can see here, a bulleted list does the following:

- ✓ Draws the reader's attention

- ✓ Helps "chunk" the information into easily grazed bits

- ✓ Enables you to efficiently highlight key information without the use of large charts and graphics

Tables

When you're presenting data that spans multiple periods or that compares the attributes of two or more items (such as competitors), that data is often best presented in tabular format.

For example, you could present the following information in a standard paragraph:

The number of U.S. wireless telephone subscribers was 69.2 million in 1998, 85.7 million in 1999, 103.7 million in 2000, and grew to 120.2 million in 2001.

It's a long, awkward sentence, and it does a good job of both burying the data and making it difficult to grasp.

A better way to present this same data would be in a table, like this:

U.S. Wireless Telephone Subscribers (Millions)

1998	1999	2000	2001
69.2	85.7	103.7	120.2

If you're using Microsoft Word to write and format your document, you can create some very sophisticated table formats; including tables with shaded backgrounds and shadowed borders—to match other graphical elements in your plan document. You can also format your table with a different font from your body text; using a smaller, simpler font (such as Arial) will enable you to conserve space on the page. See the following figure for an example of how to incorporate a sophisticated table within the text of your Opportunity section.

Charts and Graphs

For the most important and most complex data in your Opportunity section, consider presenting it in chart or graph format. A graph lets you present multiple layers of information in a single space and attracts the reader's eye.

Pictures and Graphics

If you're looking to add visual interest to your plan document, consider adding a few photographs or drawings, as appropriate. For example, you can use photographs to accompany descriptions of key products or use drawings to illustrate important processes or concepts.

Market Strategy

If you did an excellent job writing the Opportunity section of your plan, you've left your reader with one critical question: How does your company plan to take advantage of this enormous opportunity?

The answer to this question is presented in the business plan's Market Strategy section. This section walks the reader through the products and services you intend to bring to market, describes how you intend to bring them to market (in terms of both sales and marketing), and discusses the competition you'll face in the marketplace.

The Market Strategy section, more than any other part of your business plan, describes what your business does from an external perspective. You don't go into how your products are developed or manufactured (that's for the Business Strategy section) or even how you intend to make money from your activities (also in the Business Strategy section); you focus on what you're doing, in terms of products and services, to take advantage of the large market opportunity before you.

Building Your Market Strategy

The Market Strategy of your plan describes how your company intends to pursue the opportunity presented in the previous section. Typically, you will pursue an opportunity by executing the following activities:

- ✓ Develop one or more new products or services to offer to the market.

- ✓ Price, package, and position the product(s)/service(s), uniquely and competitively.

- ✓ Place the product(s)/service(s) in one or more channels of distribution that best reach the target consumer. This may involve selling directly to the consumer or through two- or three-step distribution.

✓ Promote the product(s)/service(s) to the target consumer.

✓ When you describe how your firm will execute these four activities, you've described your market strategy.

Writing the Market Strategy Section

Your first step in writing the Market Strategy section of your plan is to create an outline of the major subsections within the section. A good course of action is to use a three- or four-part outline, incorporating the three main components of your market strategy plus an optional fourth section that discusses how your product(s)/service(s) stacks up against competing product(s)/service(s). Your outline should incorporate further subsections, as necessary,

148

to deal with issues specific to your particular market strategy.

Your outline should follow the flow of your main story, which starts with the big market opportunity you discussed in the Opportunity section. You now tell the reader that you're going to take advantage of the opportunity by producing one or more new products, and you tell how they're positioned, priced, and packaged (the Product section in your Market Strategy outline); you describe how and where you're going to sell the products (the Sales and Distribution section); you discuss how you'll market and promote the products (the Marketing section), and you end by discussing how your products will compete with other products already on the market (the Competitive Comparison section).

The Product

The product you sell or the service you offer is your business. To have an effective business plan, you have to do a perfect job of presenting your product; not only what it is and what it does, but also how it compares to other similar products on the market.

This is why the first part of your response to the market as mentioned earlier opportunity should present in appropriate detail, your company's key products or services.

Defining Product

The Product part of the Market Strategy section should focus on the most essential products and services offered by your company—your flagship products, as it were. Don't include every product or service you offer; focus on the one or two products, or product categories that define your company.

For example, Microsoft wouldn't list the hundreds of products it offers in a Product section of its business plan. Microsoft would most likely define its product as "software" (not "Excel" or "Word" or "Windows") and describe, in general terms, its strategy for developing, selling, and marketing its software. Along the same lines, Honda might define its product as "automotive vehicles," and Paramount might define its product as "movies." None of these companies would focus on individual products, only on the overall category of product that it offers.

It's important to note that, in some cases, your "product" is actually your entire business. This is especially true of retail and wholesale businesses, in which you provide a service to customers by offering them a variety of products to purchase. So you don't want to discuss all the products you sell in the Product section; you want to discuss your entire business as a single product/service. For example, if you're Office

Max, your product is a chain of office-supply superstores that exploits an opportunity in the market for office supplies; if you're a local video store, your product is your store, and it utilises an opportunity in the market for video entertainment.

The Three Ps: Positioning, Pricing, And Packaging

When you start writing the Product part of your Market Strategy section, begin by introducing each product; present the name of the product and its general function (what it does). Then, in separate subsections, you should discuss the following three Ps:

- **Positioning:** This describes your product's unique features that make it different from other products or uniquely suited to exploit the market opportunity. (If you're a retailer offering a variety of products, use this point to discuss how you're positioning your store vs competing stores.)

- **Pricing:** This is a straightforward presentation of the product's pricing strategy; the product's suggested price and why you chose it. If you sell a variety of products, you can discuss the strategy behind the range of prices you've selected (good-better-best, for example), or you can discuss your overall pricing philosophy (always offer the lowest prices, for example).

- **Packaging:** If you sell your product at retail, discuss any unique aspects to the product's packaging, such as size or colour or shape. (If you don't sell at retail, ignore this point.)

Sales and Distribution

Once you've presented your product, you can discuss how you intend to present that product to potential consumers. If you sell directly to your customers, you should discuss how you reach those customers and how you execute a typical sale. If you sell to customers via the Internet, you should discuss your Web site strategy. If you sell via telemarketing, you should discuss where you get your lists and the kind of close rates you project. If you sell via retail, you should discuss what types of retailers stock your product and how you get your product to them (either directly or through distributors).

This section is where you can and should go into some detail about your company's distribution model. For example, if you're a book publisher, you would describe how you sell your books directly to some large accounts but use independent distributors to reach most smaller accounts. Describing your distribution model in words might suffice, but you also may want to include some sort of diagram to illustrate the process.

When you're describing your distribution model, it's okay to name names— that is, to mention by name the major distributors and retailers that carry your product. If you're in an existing business, putting some numbers behind the names might also be a good idea. List the top five accounts or retailers or distributors (or whatever), along with their market share, total revenues, total units shipped, or other relevant data. (A table is a good way to present this information.)

If you employ one or more sales forces to sell your product, use the Sales and Distribution section to provide a brief description of each sales force. For example, if you use different sales forces to sell your products into mass merchants and direct to government agencies, devote separate subheads to your mass merchant and government sales forces. Use a paragraph or two to describe the size and shape of each sales force, without going into unnecessary detail about commissions and structure and the like.

Note that the Sales and Distribution section is not the place to discuss how you intend to compensate your salespeople (that can go in the Operations section if you feel it's important enough to include the plan). It is also not the place to discuss the painful details of your discount schedule. Although you might want to mention an average discount, a range of cuts, or anything that investors might perceive as being out of the ordinary about the way you discount.

Marketing

Now that you've presented your product and described how you get it to your customers, you should spend a page or so discussing how you intend to get the product noticed. In other words, how you intend to market your product.

The marketing of your product can take several forms and comprise many different types of activities. Depending on your business, you may want to discuss some or all of the following activities (under separate subheads) in the Marketing section:

- **Advertising:** Advertising is just that—the paid advertising you undertake for your product or business, in whatever media you use. Your advertising might consist of print advertisements, radio spots, television ads, or online banner advertisements. You may want to segment your advertising by type of media, by national vs local, by region, by the audience (consumer vs trade), by intent (product-focused vs corporate), or by whatever factors are relevant in your particular situation.

- **Promotion:** Promotion is a separate activity from advertising. Promotion involves sales, discounts, coupons, special deals, and big campaigns, all designed to move more product. Certain types of advertising (not image advertising!) can be a component of promotion but not vice versa. If you're not sure what to include here, ask yourself this question: "What are we doing to promote our product?"

- **Public Relations:** P.R. is often characterized as free advertising, even though it's not free, and it's not advertising. It's often difficult to describe specific P.R. activities in a business plan, so this section is typically short and somewhat generic.

- **Trade Shows:** Attendance at trade shows and conferences are crucial to the success of some types of businesses. If this describes your business, you'll want to devote a subhead to your planned activities in this regard.

- **Catalogues:** If your business is catalogue-based, you'll need to discuss in detail how you execute this part of your operation. How many catalogues a year you send out, to how many customers, and what kind of response rate you get.

- **Direct Mail:** The same detail is needed here as was needed for catalogue-based businesses. Discuss how many mailings a year you intend to do, how many pieces you intend to mail, your projected response rate, the average cost of each mailing, and so on.

- **Marketing Materials:** If your business produces large numbers of brochures, point-of-purchase displays, and other assorted marketing materials, spend a paragraph or so discussing the types of materials you produce, how the materials are used, and how much money you spend on them for a year.

- **Online Marketing:** Many businesses today devote a part of their marketing budget to Internet-based marketing. Describe your online activities; your Web site, the advertising you do on other Web sites, and any other online marketing activities you engage in.

Business Strategy

Key to the Business Strategy section is the presentation of your business model; exactly how you intend to generate revenues and profits. It is this section that will convey both your business savvy and your overall goals for what your business will become.

Defining Your Business Model

For many potential investors, your business model is the crucial part of your business plan. Your business model describes how you intend to build your business, and it represents what is unique about your business. Different companies can (and will) approach the same opportunities with similar products and services; it's how you bring those products to life, how you intend to profit from that activity, and how you intend to get from here to there that makes your business unique. Investors will analyze your business model and come to some sort of conclusion about whether you've picked the right model and whether you can accomplish what it will take to implement that business model. If your model and your plans pass muster, you'll most likely get the money you need.

Your business model describes your approach to four different issues: revenue, profit, market share, and growth. You should treat each of these issues as separate subheads underneath the main Business Model head in your plan document.

Revenue Streams

The first component of your business model is revenue. In this part of the section, then, you need to describe precisely where your revenues will come from.

If your company produces only one product or offers only one service, this section has the potential to be relatively simple. "One hundred per cent of all company revenues are generated by Product A" would be a valid approach. Unless, of course, there were other defining parameters. For example, you might sell only one product or service, but you might sell it into multiple channels or regions. In this scenario, you'd want to describe the revenues generated from each channel or region.

Obviously, if you produce multiple products or product lines, or if your revenues are split between different products and services, you need to describe each major source of revenue. The defining parameters for each revenue stream should be noted in your text; important characteristics might include any or all of the following:

- Product
- Price
- Discount rate

- Sales cost

- Type of sales force or sales vehicle employed

- Amount of marketing and advertising necessary

- Intensity of competition

- Length of the sales cycle

In short, you need to point out any significant differences between your revenue streams.

Not only do you need to describe each revenue stream, but you also need to quantify it. For the Business Strategy section, describing each stream in terms of percentage of total revenues (as opposed to showing actual revenues by stream) is the preferred method. This way, potential lenders and investors can apply this revenue mix (on a percentage basis) to different total revenue numbers. (For example, if you say that revenue stream A represents 20 per cent of total revenues, the reader can do his or her math to size this stream against different projected total revenue numbers, by multiplying the total revenue by the 20-per cent share.)

An excellent way to present your revenue mix is with a pie chart (see the following figure). The visual nature of a pie chart very quickly imparts the comparative size information that is key to the revenue stream mixture. Use the narrative text to describe each revenue stream and a pie chart to show its relative size.

Profit Margins

Now that you've shown where your revenues will be coming from, it's time to discuss just how profitable you expect each revenue stream to be.

This part of the Business Model section can be relatively short. The first thing you need to do is list the projected gross margin for each revenue stream. You use gross margin (which represents your profit after cost of goods sold but before operating expenses) because it represents the direct costs of a particular product or service. Operating expenses include some amount of fixed costs, as well as costs (such as corporate overhead) that are shared between different revenue streams and thus don't accurately represent the true costs of an individual product or service.

You can present these gross margins in your text, in a table, or a horizontal bar chart (see the following figure). (Don't use a vertical bar chart; bars aligned from left to right imply the passage of time, which is not what you're presenting.) You should also devote some narrative text (a paragraph per revenue stream perhaps) to describing why one revenue stream has higher or lower gross margins than another.

Market Share

In most cases, your company's revenues are directly related to your market share. To achieve a projected revenue number, you'll have to accomplish a specific share of your market; or you'll have to generate somehow revenues from outside your market, which is difficult to plan for and explain.

Organization and Operations

So far, your business plan has discussed why you're in business (the Vision and Mission sections), has defined the market opportunity you want to pursue (Opportunity), has described how you intend to pursue that opportunity (Market Strategy) and has presented the business model you'll use to implement your market strategy (Business Strategy). Now, in the Organization and Operations section, you get to discuss, from an operational perspective, just how you'll go about executing your business strategy.

In short, the Organization and Operations section of your business plan is where you detail how your business is structured and how each part of your business (each department or business unit) works. Most companies can present this information in six pages or less, although the larger your business, the more space you'll need to devote to this section.

Outlining and Preparation

You attack the Organization and Operations section the same way you attack the rest of your business plan document; by building a detailed outline and by assembling the key information you need to flesh it out.

Building Your Outline

The outline for your Organization and Operations section splits into two distinct parts: Organization and Operations. The Organization section describes your company's structure (typically in the form of an organization chart), and the Operations section is divided into separate sections for each major department or operating unit of your business.

If a particular part of your business is key to the implementation of your specific plan, you may want to elevate that department into its section on a level with the Organization and Operations section. Just follow the simple rule that more important functions deserve more coverage, and you'll be on the right track.

Assembling the Details

What kind of detail do you need to write your plan's Organization and Operations section?

For the Organization section, you'll need a high-level org chart; show the top-level (president or owner or CEO), the next level of direct reports, and maybe (in less detail) the next level below that. While you're creating the main org chart, however, you should consider including departmental org charts for each subsection of the Organization section; you may need to get this detail from the individual departments.

An org chart isn't the only thing you need to get from each of your key departments. Since each department or operating unit gets its subhead, you'll need to

collect detailed information from each department—
what it does, how it does it, how it's organized, and so
on. It's not uncommon to devote a half page or more
to each department, which is a lot of space to fill;
especially if you don't know much about what's going
on there.

A good approach is to assign the writing of each
department's section to the departments themselves.
Ask each department for a three- to four-page
overview and then have the business plan's main
writer use those overviews to create the actual sections
for the plan document. This approach helps involve
your key managers in the business plan process,
provides the information you might have trouble
coming up with yourself, and then leaves the final
editing to a real writer.

Presenting Your Organization

The Organization part of this section is relatively easy to write. All you need is a brief introductory paragraph and an org chart.

How you approach the org chart, however, is important. You have to determine how many levels to include on the chart and how much detail to provide about each level. You also have to decide whether you want to include only departments and titles on the chart or also include the names of key managers.

Discussing Your Operations

The Operations part of your plan (sometimes called Infrastructure) is where you describe what each piece and part of your company does. This section is mainly here to show potential lenders and investors that you do have a depth of organization and that someone who knows what he or she is doing is watching over the company at that level of detail.

You should create subheads within this section for each major department, group, or operating unit. A solid strategy is that if a department or unit shows up on the second level of your corporate org chart, it needs its subhead. (Conversely, if it's important enough for its own subhead, it had better show up as a direct report to the CEO/president, or something's seriously wrong with your company's structure!)

Product Development

Whether you make or buy your products, Product Development (or whatever you call it at your company) is a fairly important part of your Operations section. Not only will you want to describe your product development department, but you'll also want to describe your product development process. You'll want to describe how you obtain new products, from conception to manufacturing; illustrating this process with a flow chart of some sort would be a good idea. You should also include data relating to the cost of development either for an average product or for your most important products.

Manufacturing

If you make your products, this is the place to discuss that process. Include a flow chart if appropriate, as well as descriptions of all your manufacturing facilities. (If you want to include a picture of some high-tech assembly line or manufacturing apparatus, it would at least serve to break up a long chunk of text.) You should also discuss product costs here, as well as any unique processes you utilize to control or reduce those costs.

Warehouse and Distribution

If you do your warehousing and distribution, talk about that department here. Make sure to include all pertinent data, including the size of your warehouse(s), the average number of days of inventory on hand, the time it takes to process a standard order, and the like.

Sales

You should have already presented your sales strategy and sales forces back in the Market Strategy section, so all you need to discuss here is the structure of the sales department itself. If you want to include a commission schedule or a discussion of compensation plans, this is the place to do it. Although that might be too much detail, even here.

Marketing

You've already presented your marketing strategy and activities (back in the Market Strategy section), so all you need to discuss here is the structure of your marketing department. You may want to present projected yearly marketing/advertising expenses if those weren't included earlier in the plan.

Information Technology

Whether you call it IT or MIS or something else, this is where you discuss the technical backbone of your company. If your company is reliant on technology, go into some detail here and include a list of the servers, software, and systems you employ. This section is especially important if you're in a high-tech industry; potential investors might examine this section to see if you have a strong enough technical infrastructure to execute the components of your plan.

Finance and Accounting

You don't have to say much about your finance, accounting, accounts receivable/payable, and related departments. Include a list of functions and an org chart, and you have it covered.

Facilities

If you operate out of a single office, this section should be short and sweet. Just describe your location, list the total space, and tell the rent you pay (either in whole or in terms of dollars per square foot). If you own several different facilities, you should list and describe each one, including the core functions at each location.

If you're a retailer, this becomes a much more critical section of your plan. You'll need to describe your facility management strategy;

how you locate new locations, how much (on average) you pay to build or rent, what kind of expense goes into getting a new site ready for operation, and so on. If you're a retailer, you may want to place this section closer to the top of the Operations section and include appropriate tables and graphs to provide the kind of detail a potential lender or investor might be looking for.

Human Relations

HR is similar to finance/accounting in that it doesn't provide a unique competitive advantage to your business. (Some HR people would disagree, of course—although the reality is that few if any business strategies revolve around the company's HR department.) Include a list of essential functions and an orgnizational chart, and you've provided more than enough information.

The Management

The Management section of your business plan has a simple structure. All you have to do is provide an introductory sentence or two and then write a short one-paragraph bio for each member of your core management team.

The introductory paragraph should stress the breadth and depth of experience that your team possesses. An excellent way to do this is to discuss the overall background of the team and the number of years of "combined experience" that everyone brings to the table. (Just add up each manager's number of years in the workplace.)

Writing A Compelling Bio

Once you're past the introduction, you face the task of writing bios for each of the key individuals on your management team. Each bio should be relatively short (no more than a paragraph in length) and should include a handful of key information points.

The bios you write for each manager should focus on information relevant to your business and his or her assigned duties. You don't need or want to include all the information that might be included in personal resumés; think about what might impress your potential lenders and investors and focus on those points.

For example, you want to mention previous job experience that relates to a person's current position in your company. You don't want to mention hobbies, clubs, or other outside activities that have no bearing on what the person tries to accomplish during the day.

Defining Key Management

There are no hard-and-fast rules about who gets into the plan and who doesn't. Just because an individual is a direct report to the president doesn't mean he or she should necessarily be included; just because someone isn't a direct report doesn't exclude him or her either.

In general, you should include bios for individuals who meet the following criteria:

- Have a strategic impact on the business

- Are crucial to the day-to-day management of the company

- Have daily interaction with the owner/president/CEO

- Are likely to have contact with investors or the board of directors

In most companies, this means that the owner/president/CEO and all direct reports get included. Key high-level staff members might also make the list, as might selected middle management. You will most likely end up with 6 to 10 bios from your management team.

Including the Board of Directors

If your company has a board of directors, you may want to include a list of board members in your Management section. If you do so, you probably want to list the board separate from your management team.

Core Competencies and Challenges

Presenting Your Strengths and Weaknesses

There are several reasons to incorporate a Core Competencies and Challenges section in your business plan document:

- Summarizing your unique competitive advantages in a single section serves to highlight and remind readers about those unique aspects of your business strategy.

- Ending the text part of your plan with a list of your strengths is a great way to end your plan; you leave your readers with a summary of the key points you want them to remember.

- By bringing up potential objections before your audience does (in the Challenges section), you preempt some tough questions and can address these issues on your terms.

- When you answer potential challenges with distinct strategies, you turn your weaknesses into strengths, and present yourself as being both realistic and proactive.

In other words, including a Core Competencies and Challenges section permits you to focus the reader's attention on the issues that you deem most important.

If you decide to include the Core Competencies and Challenges section in your business plan document, there are several options to choose from in terms of the presentation of information. These options are discussed next.

Presenting Core Competencies

If you think of the Core Competencies section as a summary of your business's unique competitive advantages, you'll agree that this section should be no more than one page in length and include a half-dozen or so separate points. Approach this section as you would a summary, and you'll start on the right track.

Choosing Your Strengths

Which strengths should you choose to include in the Core Competencies section? Here are some tips:

- The strengths should be of major import to the success of your business strategy. Being able to negotiate terrific pricing on pens and paper is a good thing, but it won't impact the success of your strategy one iota.

- The strengths should be immediately visible. This means you're most likely looking at marketplace or external strengths rather than internal operational strengths. This isn't a hard and fast rule though; if you have internal operations that enable you to reduce the cost and selling price of your product or to bring your product to market faster, then that internal strength should be noted.

- The strengths should be unique. If you note that you can bring a product to market in five days, but all your competitors also have a five-day delivery, then your strength isn't unique and shouldn't be included in this section.

- The strengths should be real. In no instance should you claim an advantage you don't truely possess. Above all else, your business plan document should be truthful; even the littlest of white lies can come back to haunt you big time.

Writing About Your Strengths

How do you write about your company's strengths without it sounding like unmitigated bragging? Here are some points to keep in mind:

- ✓ **Turn your features into benefits:** It's always tempting to talk about what you do rather than what you do for the customer. You need to go beyond presenting the key features of your business to discuss how those features benefit your customers.

- ✓ **State the facts, but don't brag:** There's no need to exaggerate the facts. State what it is you offer without undue embellishment; avoid the temptation to brag about your strengths, and allow your readers to draw their conclusions.

- ✓ **Be concise:** At this point in the business plan document, your readers are ready to call it a day and don't want to be bombarded with yet another long and detailed section. Make each advantage fit within a single paragraph or bullet point and keep it short enough to be easily grazable by your readers.

- ✓ **Highlight the key point:** You can enhance gradability by stating the specific advantage in the first sentence of the paragraph and then boldfacing that sentence.

- ✓ **Compare to competitors:** For your competitive advantage to be unique, you must compare it to what your competitors offer. If you do X, spend a sentence pointing out that your competitors do Y; and that customers prefer X to Y.

Presenting Challenges

The challenges to your business are very real and extremely important, which is why they need to be addressed in your business plan document. However, you need to present these challenges in a fashion that doesn't scare away potential lenders and investors; if at all possible, you need to present these challenges in a way that inspires additional confidence in your management abilities.

Choosing Your Challenges

If you want your Challenges section to be no more than a page in length (and shorter is probably better), then you can only include four or five distinct points. Your criteria for deciding which challenges to include should be the mirror image of your criteria for choosing strengths:

- The challenges should have a major potential impact on the success of your business strategy. The fact that your chief competitor offers free soft drinks to all its employees might be interesting, but it's not strategically significant.

- The challenges should be immediately visible. This means that you're most likely looking at marketplace challenges, such as higher-quality or lower-cost products, rather than your competitors' internal operational strengths.

- The challenges should be unique. If your competitors all offer special pricing to certain accounts, and you do too—then it's a competitive wash.

- The challenges should have a real impact. Sometimes it looks as if a competitor is doing something truly unique in the marketplace—but unless that activity results in additional revenues or profits, it really doesn't count.

In short, you need to identify four or five things that your competitors are doing better than you are and that have a measurable impact on marketplace performance. These are your true competitive challenges and need to be addressed.

Turning Challenges into Strengths

Just listing your challenges isn't enough; you need to tell your readers how you're going to respond to those challenges. If all you do is list your problems without solutions—you come off as both problematic and ineffectual.

Here is some advice to follow when writing about your company's challenges:

- **Identify the challenge:** Don't beat around the bush; get everything out in the open from the start by identifying the problem in the first sentence.

- **Quantify the problem:** If you can quantify the potential impact of the problem (in terms of revenues, profits, customer counts, market share, or whatever), then you should include that number in the text.

- **Get to the root of the problem:** Once you've identified and quantified the problem, discuss what factors are contributing to the issue. Maybe it's something you're doing that you shouldn't be; maybe it's something you should be doing that you're not; maybe it's something your competitors are doing that you can't. Whatever it is, get it out into the open quickly.

- **Strategize a solution:** Once the challenge is identified, tell the reader how you intend to respond to it. You can try to minimize the impact; you can try to equalize the playing field; you can pledge to improve your performance. Whatever it is after you've set up the problem, present your solution— positively and succinctly.

This last point is the most important. You not only have to identify potential challenges; you have to convince your readers that you have a plan to do something about them. Raise an issue and then address an issue; identify a problem, and then propose a solution. That's the key to shifting the Challenges section from a painful listing of problems into a reassuring reflection of your management savvy.

Financials

The final section of your business plan document is the Financials section. This is where you present the past, present, and future financial statements of your business.

In a way, the Financials section defines the goals you have for your business. The revenues and profits you project for future years are your company's financial goals. In essence, they're the yardstick with which you'll measure the success of your business strategy over the next several years.

Even though this section of your plan is only a few pages long, it's important enough to warrant significant attention on your part. Not only must the historical numbers be accurate, but the future financials should also be believable, achievable, and in synch, with the rest of the story, you're telling through the business plan. Given this importance, it takes time to get the numbers just right; and to present them in a fashion that has the most impact on your audience.

What Financials to Include

When preparing the Financials section of your plan, the first thing to decide is which financial statements to include. If you add too much information, you'll overwhelm the readers and dilute the impact of your most important financial goals. If you include too little information, you'll raise more questions than you answer.

Core Financial Statements

Although every business is different, there are a handful of basic financial statements that you should consider including in the Financials section of your business plan document. While you should consult with potential lenders and investors to find out what numbers they expect to see, chances are the list will include some or all of the following:

- **Revenue projection:** Not all businesses need to include a revenue projection separate from that in the pro forma income statements, but if your business generates revenues from a complex assortment of sources, breaking down your projections by type of revenue might be a good idea.

- **Income statements:** One or more income statements are virtual requirements for the vast majority of business plans. A pro forma income statement projecting forward at least three years is a necessity for both old and new businesses. If you're running an existing business, you should also include current and historical (going back at least three years) income statements.

- **Balance sheet:** If you're just starting up your business, you obviously won't need to include a balance sheet, but if you're running an existing business; and especially if you're presenting to bankers or other lenders. A current balance sheet should be included. (In some rare occasions a projected balance sheet might also be necessary, especially if you're asking for asset-based financing.)

- **Cash flow projection:** Larger investors might not be interested in your cash flow requirements, but lenders will be—as will some smaller investors.

In what order should these financial statements flow? As always, you can control the order best to fit the demands of your audience and your business. However, the normally accepted order for these documents would be as follows:

1. Revenue projection (if included)

2. Income statement projection

3. Income statement current (if included)

4. Income statement historical (if included)

5. Balance sheet (if included)

6. Cash flow projection (if included)

All projected financial statements should be accompanied by a list of the assumptions used to construct the numbers. These assumptions can be in the form of footnotes or endnotes and can (and probably should) be presented in an extremely low-key fashion; this means smaller type without a lot of fancy formatting.

There are other types of financial statements that, though less-frequently used, you may need to include in your particular business plan. These could include a breakeven analysis, a listing of your capital assets, and other similar documents. Include these if specifically requested to by a potential lender or investor.

Chapter Four

The Navigation:

- ❖ Table of Contents
- ❖ Page Numbering

Table of Contents and Index

At this point, we will assume you've written the first draft of your business plan document. We'll also assume you used some version of Microsoft Word to do the writing and that your business plan is contained in a Word document file. (Even if you used a different word processing program, such as WordPerfect, the navigational and formatting features should be similar.) Now it's time to start thinking about what the final form of your document will look like.

The concept of document navigation concerns the ability to find the things you want to see within a longer document. One reader might want to go directly to some vital market information or jump straight to the financial statements; another might want to find information relating to a particularly hot topic. The easier it is to find specific details, the more useful your business plan will be. It's definitely in your best interest to incorporate elements that improve the navigability of your document.

The Elements of Navigation

If you have a concise document; a half-dozen pages or less, elements specific to navigation aren't essential; the document is short enough to thumb through and find anything you might be specifically looking for. With longer documents, however, it becomes increasingly more difficult to find information just by flipping through the pages.

In the case of your business plan, you have a document that is 20 or more pages in length, possibly much longer when you factor in appendixes. It would be expecting too much to ask your readers to reference specific information by scanning page after page after page; instead, you need to offer additional routes into your document to facilitate direct access to particular information.

The most basic navigational element is the page number. All other navigation elements depend on the presence of page numbers because they reference specific numbered pages. So if you do nothing else, make sure you number your pages!

When you're dealing with documents the size of your business plan, it's a good idea to organize the information into distinct sections, which you do by using varying levels of heads and subheads. This way, the information flows smoothly from top to bottom, and when using Word's Outline view, you can visually see just how your document is organized.

If you've organized your document properly, you can create a kind of outline view for your readers by adding a table of contents (TOC) at the front of your document. The TOC lists the heads and specified subheads within your document, along with the page numbers of each section. A reader wanting to find a specific section of your document need only reference the TOC and then turn to the appropriate page.

Finally, some business plans will incorporate an index of important topics and terms. The index is located at the very end of the document and lists the keywords and phrases used, along with the page numbers indicating where those words and phrases appear. A reader looking for a specific topic—market size, let's say; would look up that topic in the index and then turn to the page(s) where that topic appears.

You don't have to incorporate all (or any) of these navigation elements in your specific plan. Note, however, that the less navigation you accommodate, the more likely it is that your readers won't be able to reference key information, and we all know that dissatisfied readers diminish your plan's chances for success. Smart businesspeople embrace any opportunity to make their business plans more effective; adding navigational elements is a relatively easy task that can generate untold benefits.

Adding Page Numbers

The most straightforward navigational element to add to your business plan document is numbered pages. Page numbers are typically incorporated in the header or footer and can help readers find their place as they read through your document.

You can add page numbers to your document manually or automatically.

Manual Page Numbers

If your document includes subsidiary documents inserted within the normal page flow, you may need to number your pages manually. You can add manual page numbers in several different ways, including the following:

- Hand numbering—recommended only if you have very neat hand-writing

- Stamps, using some sort of ink stamping device

- Press-on numbers

- Using a typewriter to type numbers at the bottom of each page

Automatic Page Numbers

A simpler and more versatile approach is to number the pages automatically within Microsoft Word. Not only can Word add page numbers (and update them interactively), the program can also use the page numbers to link to other navigational elements such as tables of contents and indexes. You will typically place page numbers in the header or footer of your document, by using Word's automatic page numbering feature.

Where to Start Numbering

If you add a basic automatic page number in Microsoft Word, every page of your document will be numbered, including the title page and the table of contents page. This isn't good form.

To make your business plan look as professional as possible, you want both your title page and your TOC to be unnumbered. In other words, you want the first page of your Executive Summary to be page 1 of your document.

Give this book a review

THANK YOU